AF375052

ISBN: 978-9948-25-337-2 (Paperback)

All images are by the publisher.
Book design by the publisher.

First printing edition 2020.

Houssam Abou Taha
PO BOX 118353
Dubai, UAE

hktaha@gmail.com

three days in Sanaa

In March, 2006, I had a rare opportunity to visit the extraordinary city of Sanaa, Yemen. I had no idea what to expect. Luckily, I brought my camera with me (a Nikon D70s) to capture what I was about to experience over three short but very memorable days.

Sanaa has been inhabited for over 2,500 years and sits in a valey at an altitude of 2200m. In the 6th and 7th centuries, it became a major religoius and political center for Islam. The architecture of the old city, most of which was built before the 11th century, still stands to this day. It is, in fact, still a bustling city, with over 6000 houses, mosques, old souks and many labyrinths. It is an outstanding example of homogenous architecture influenced by early Islamic art, which is distinguished for its beautiful and intricate geometric patterns.

It is no wonder, then, that Sanaa's old city is a UNESCO World Heritage site.

I hope you enjoy these images as much as I did making them.

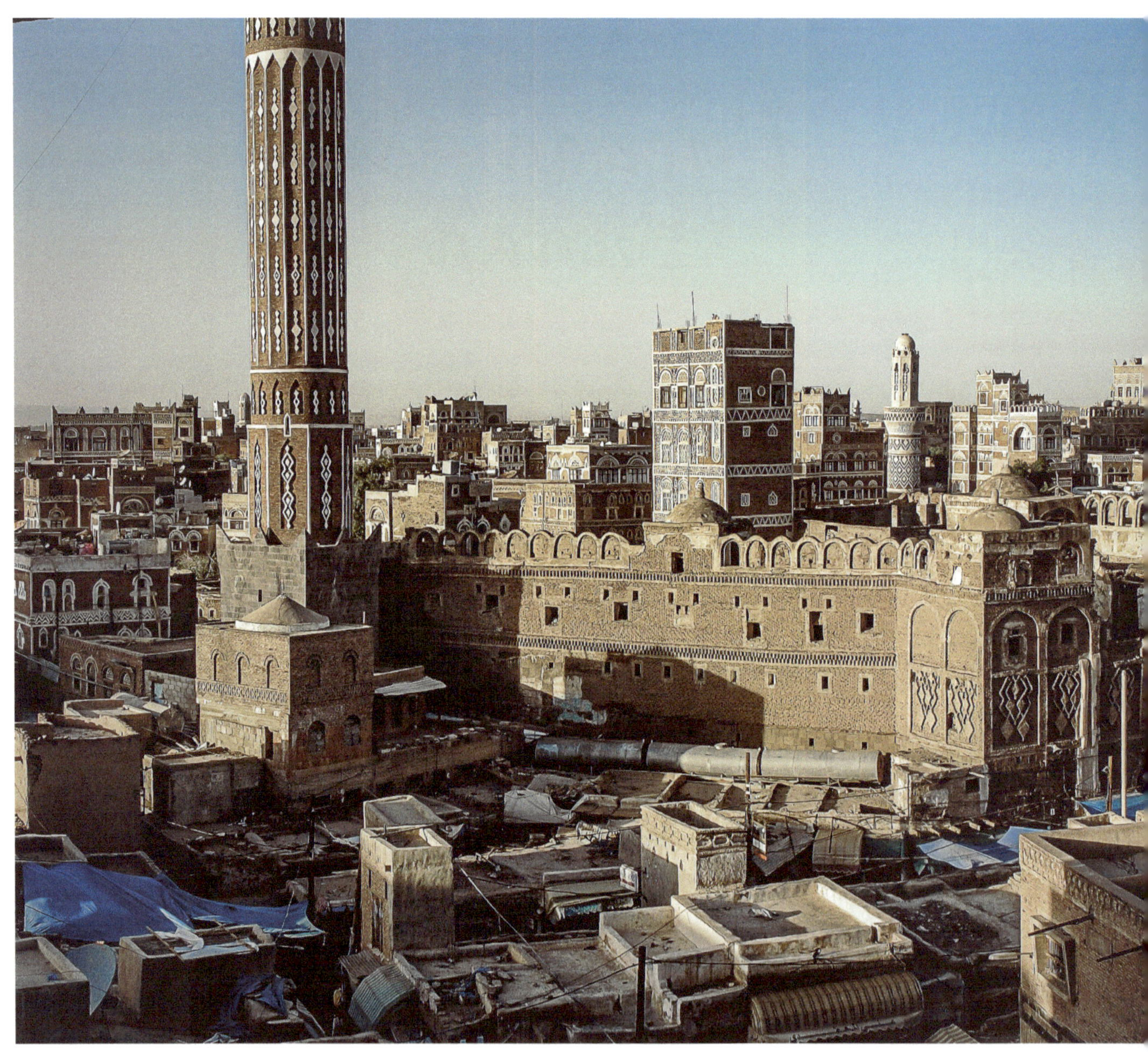

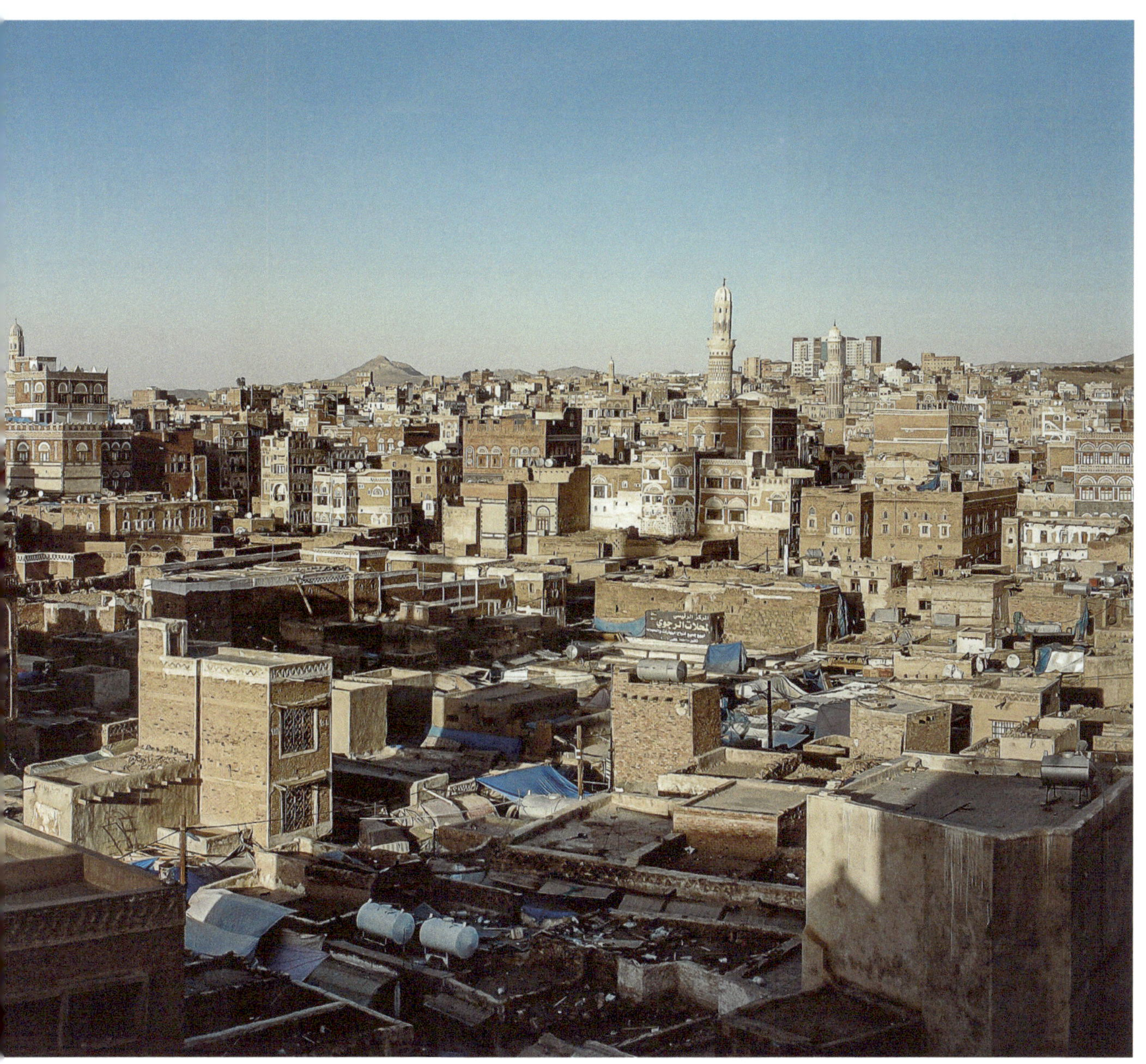

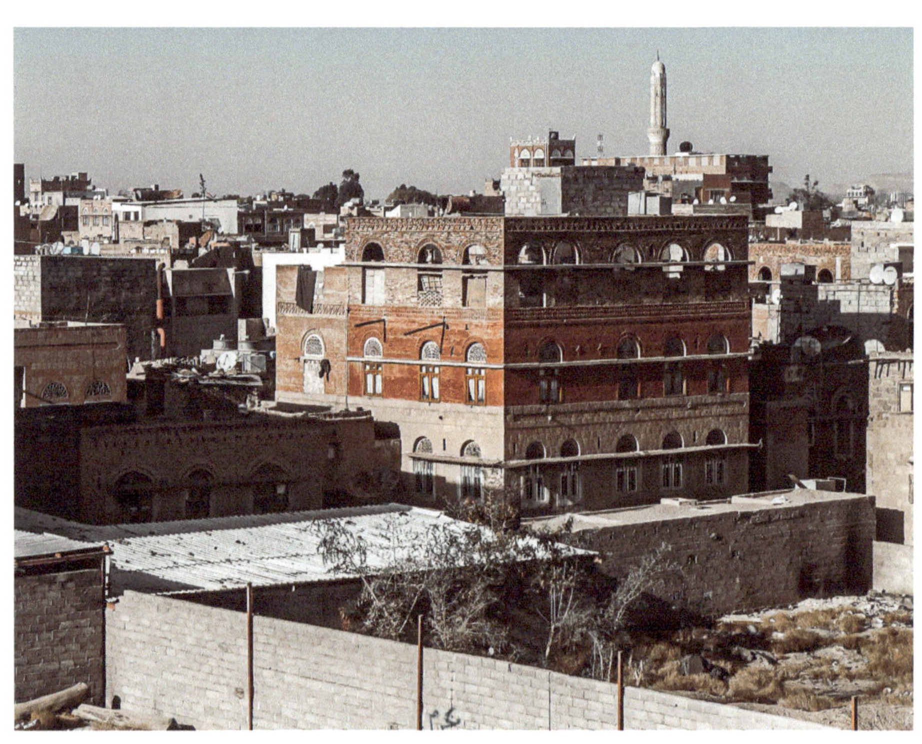

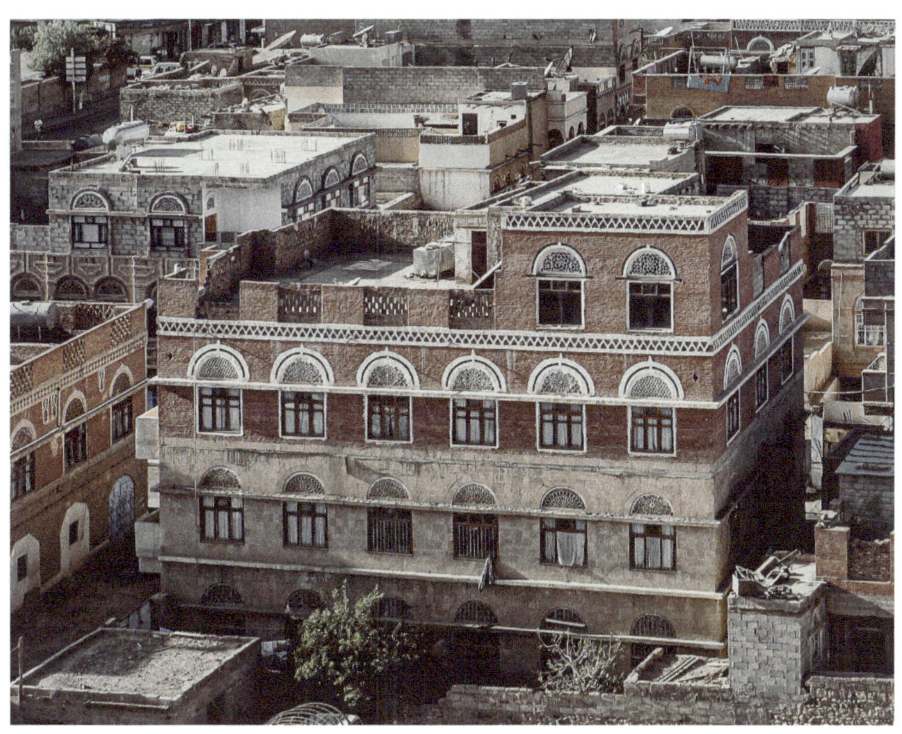

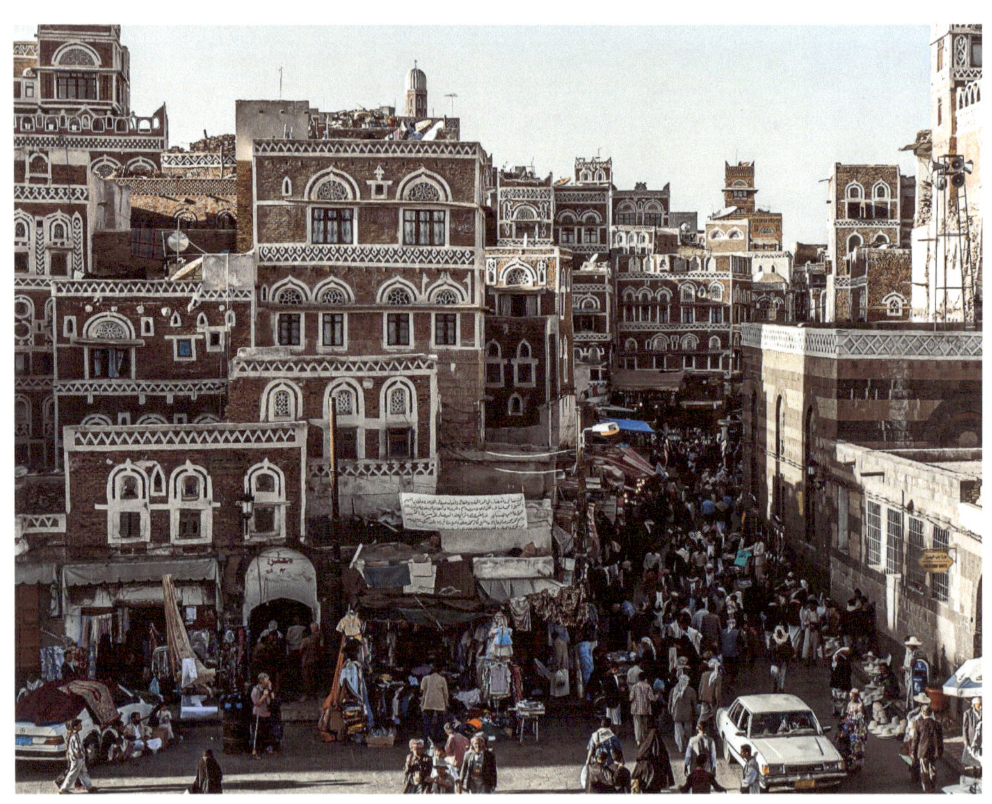

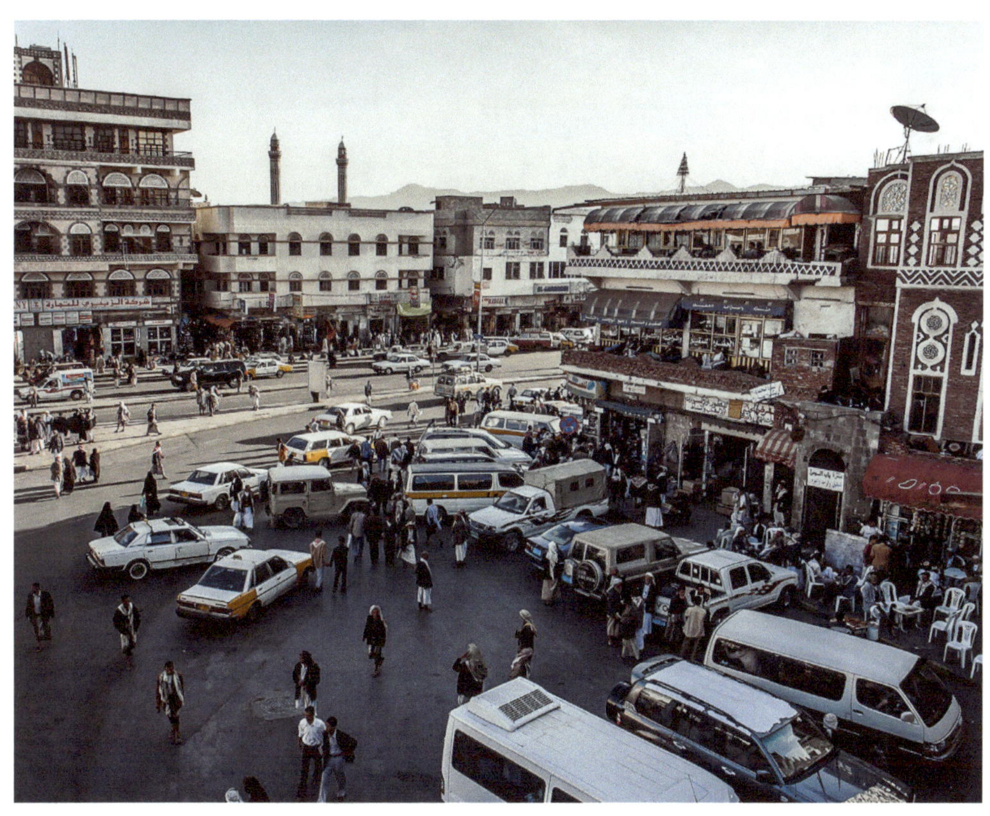

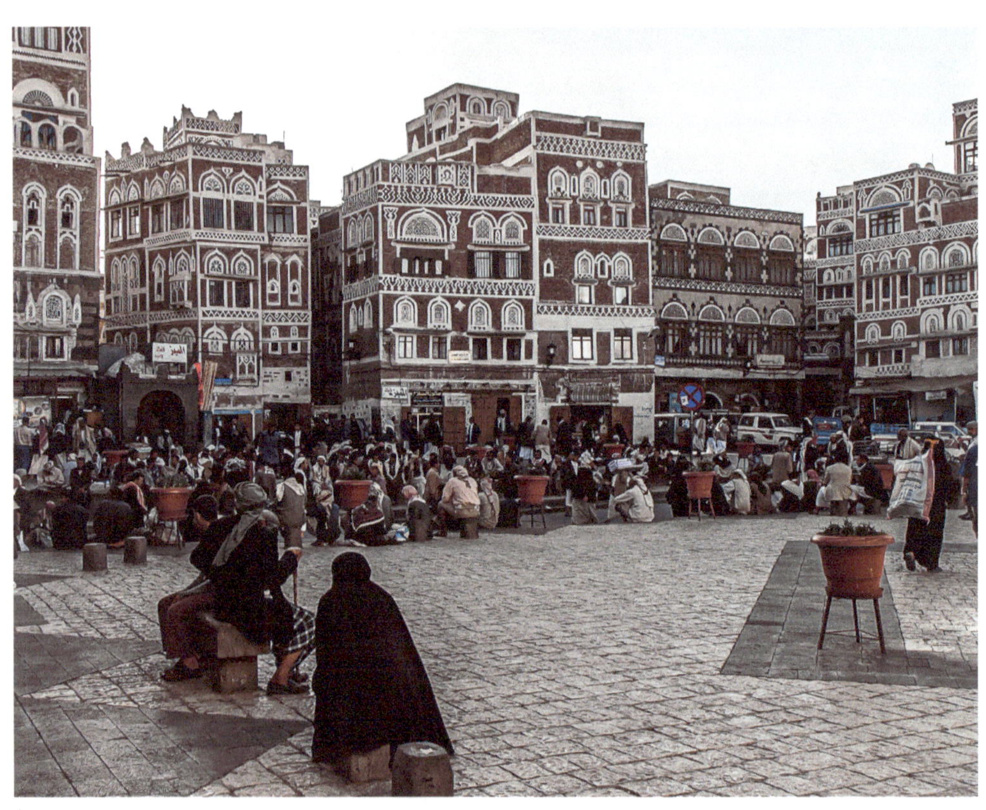

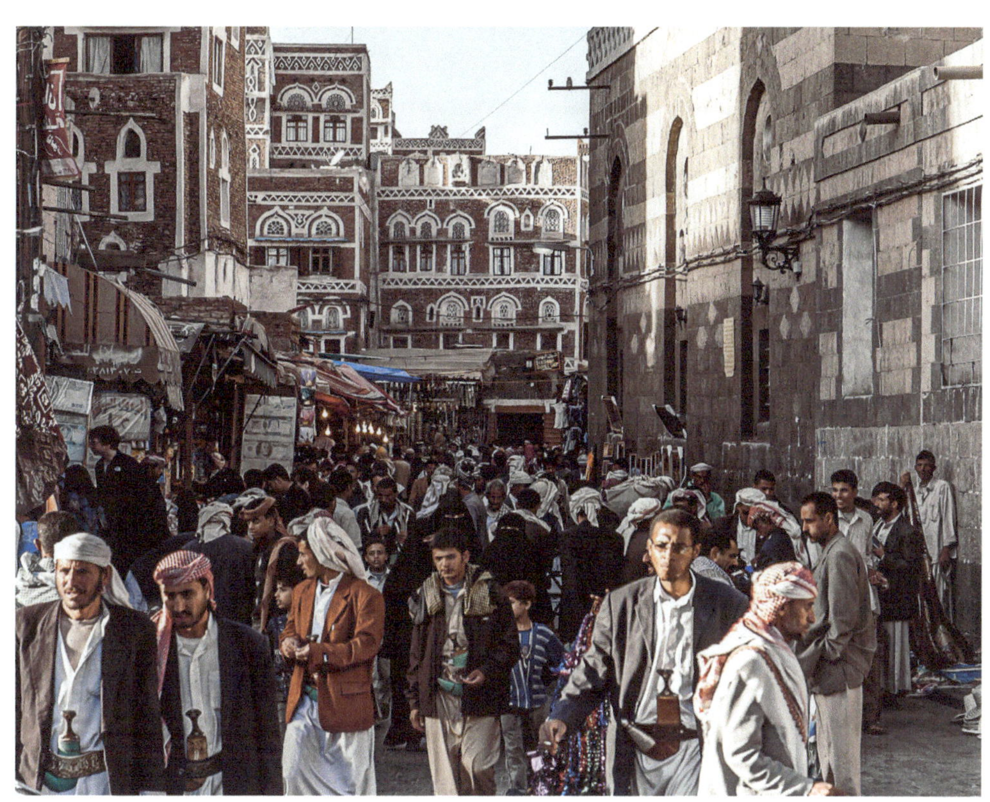

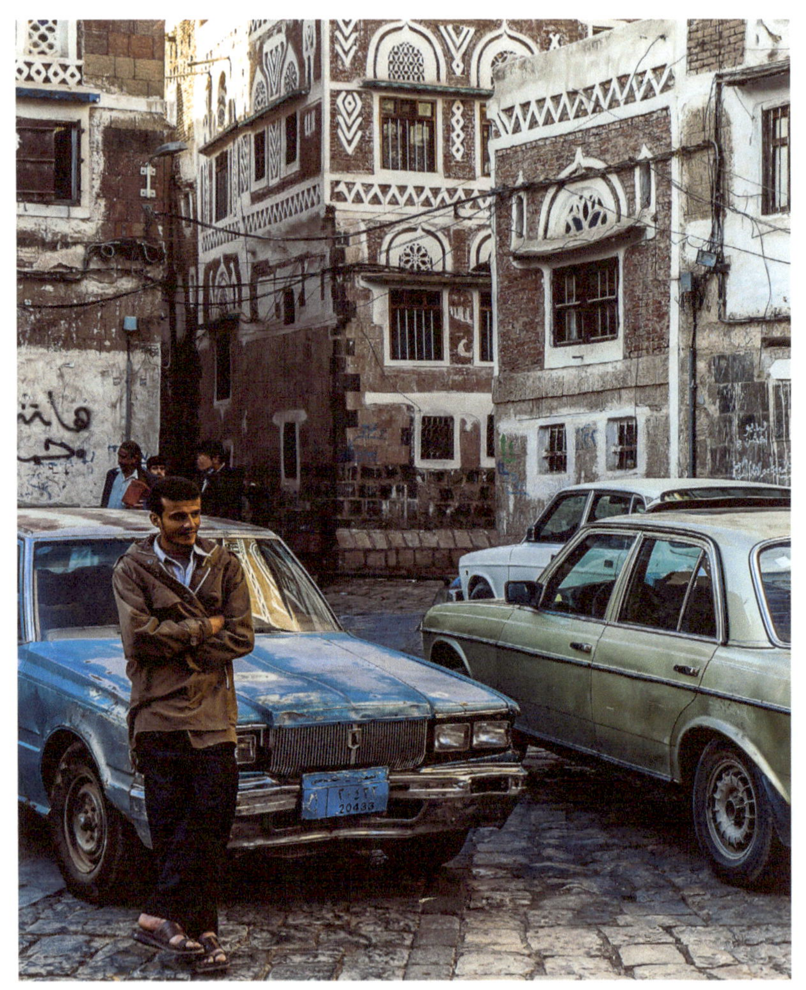

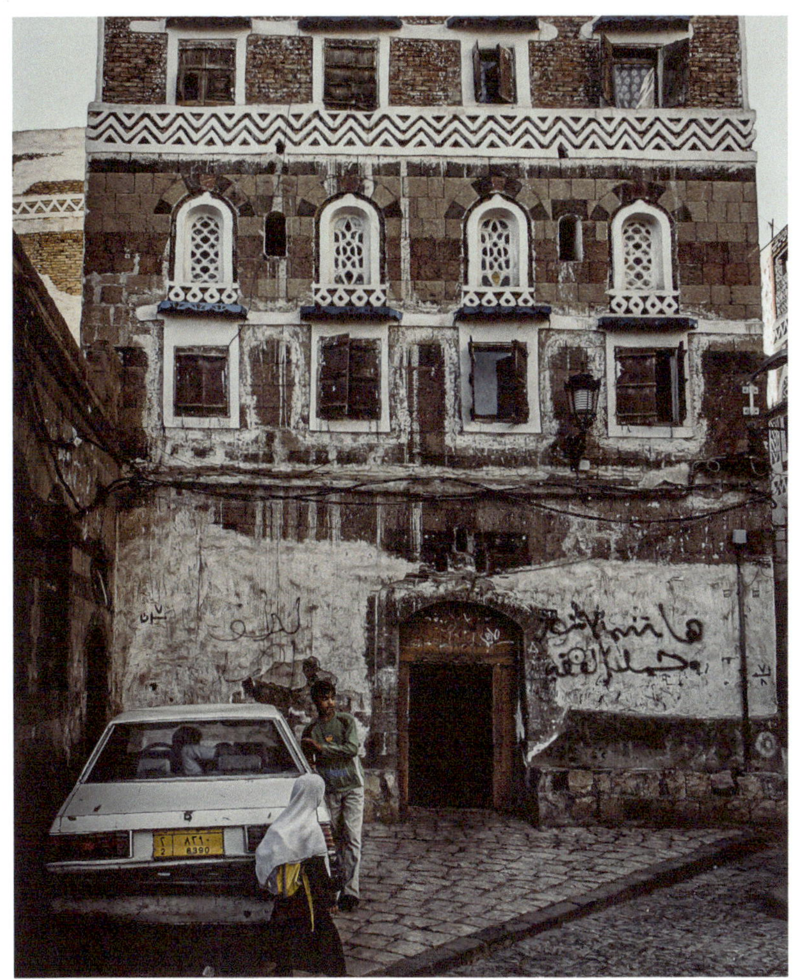

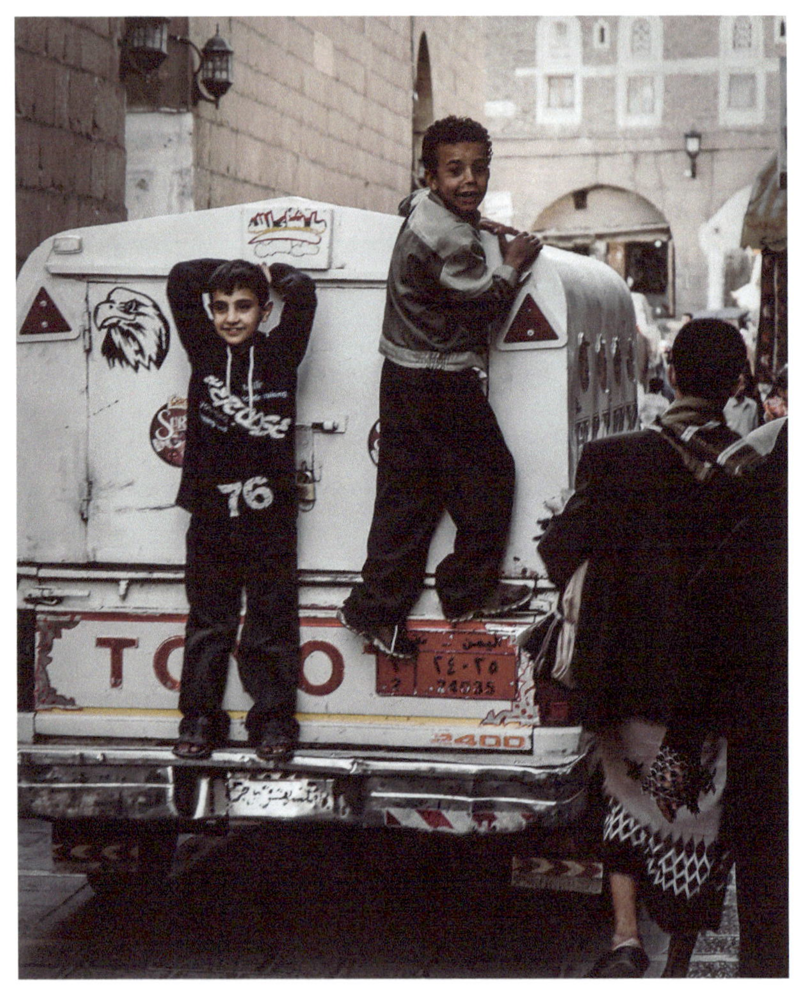

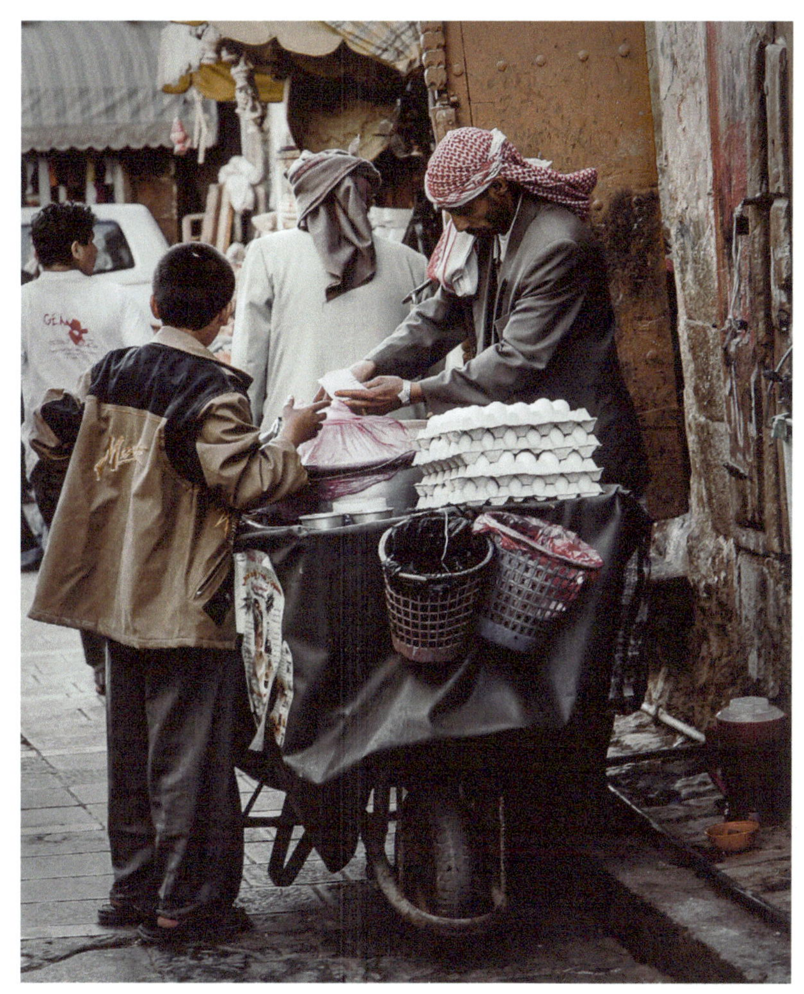

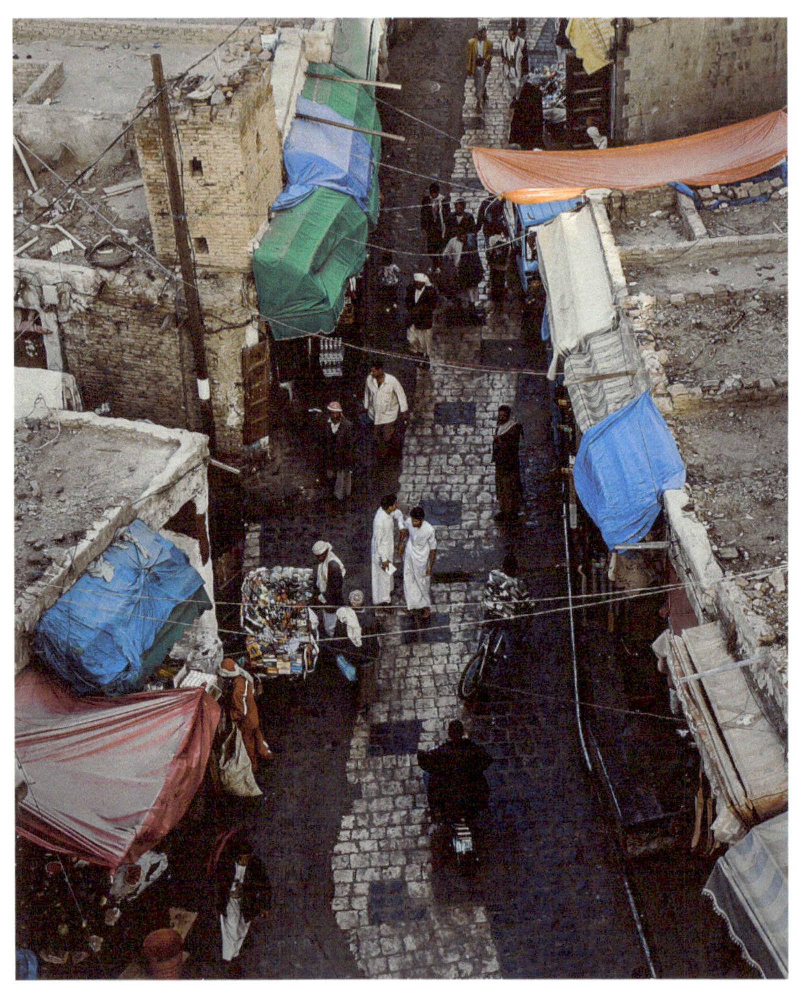

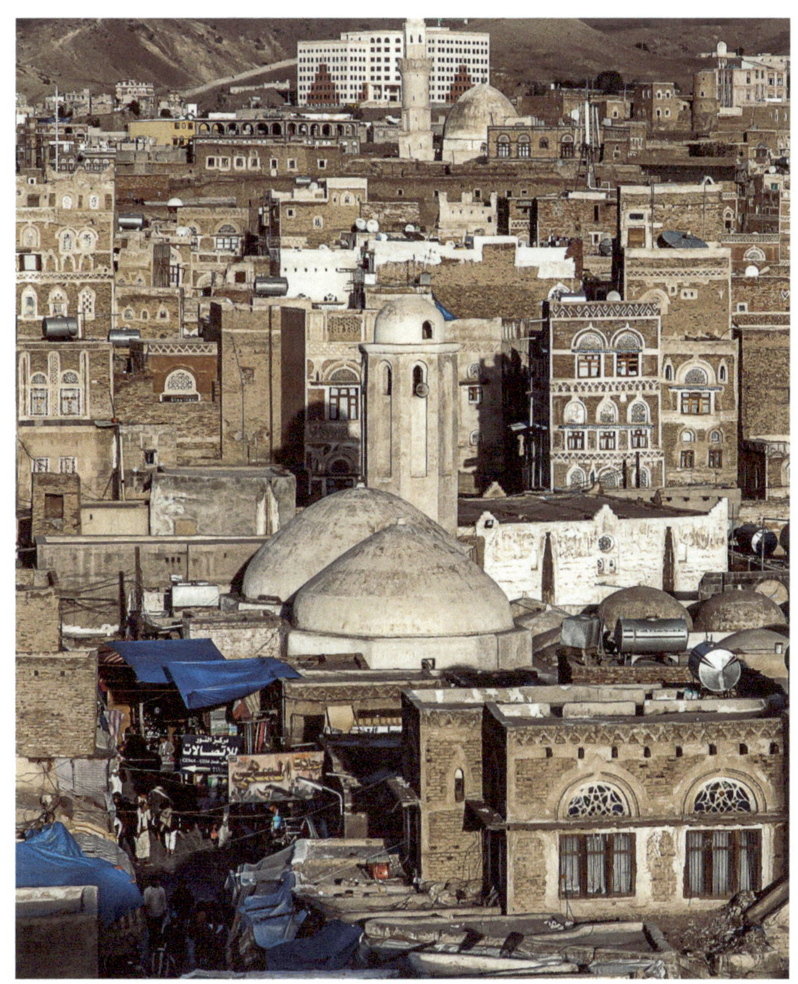

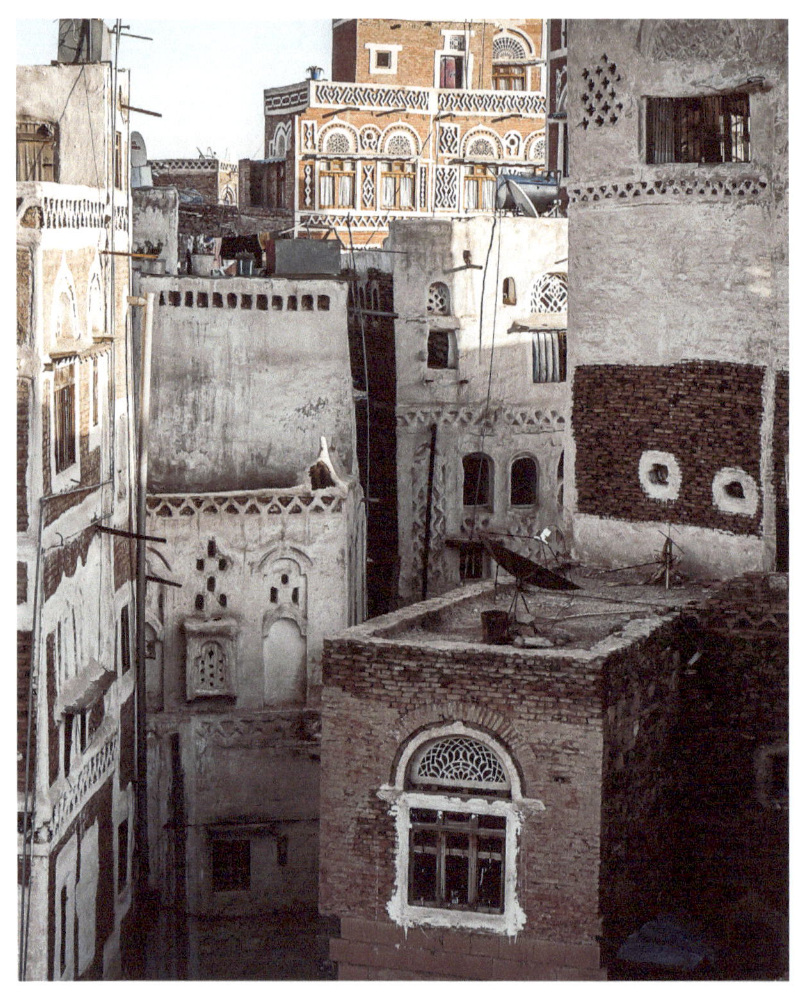

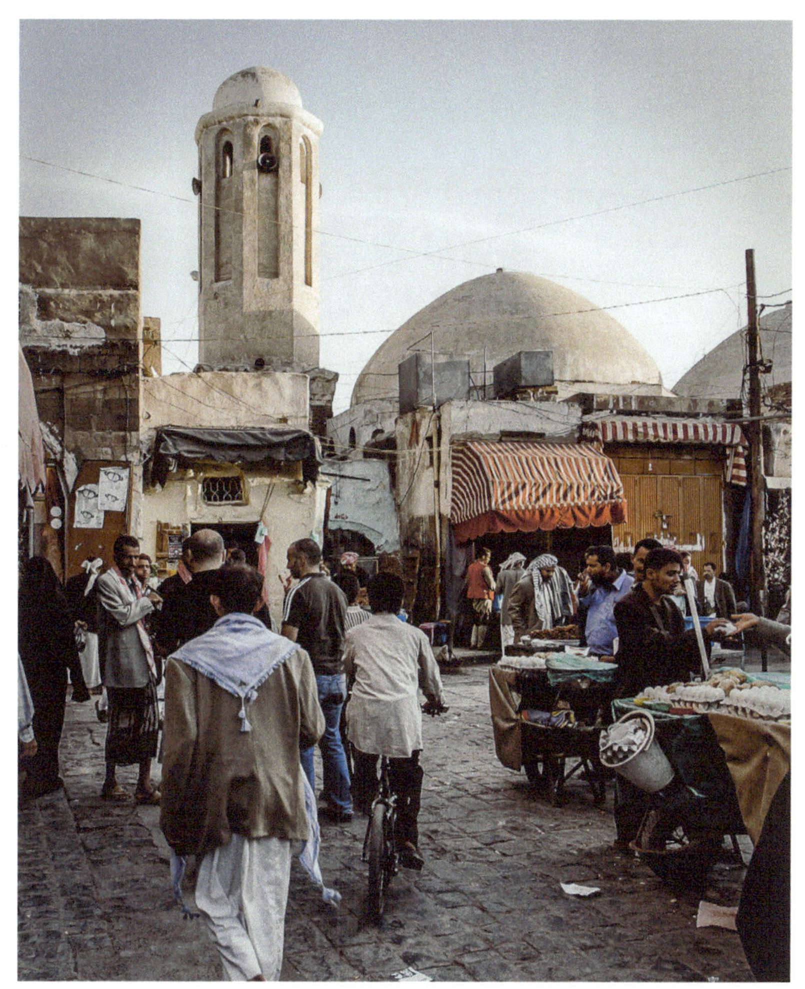

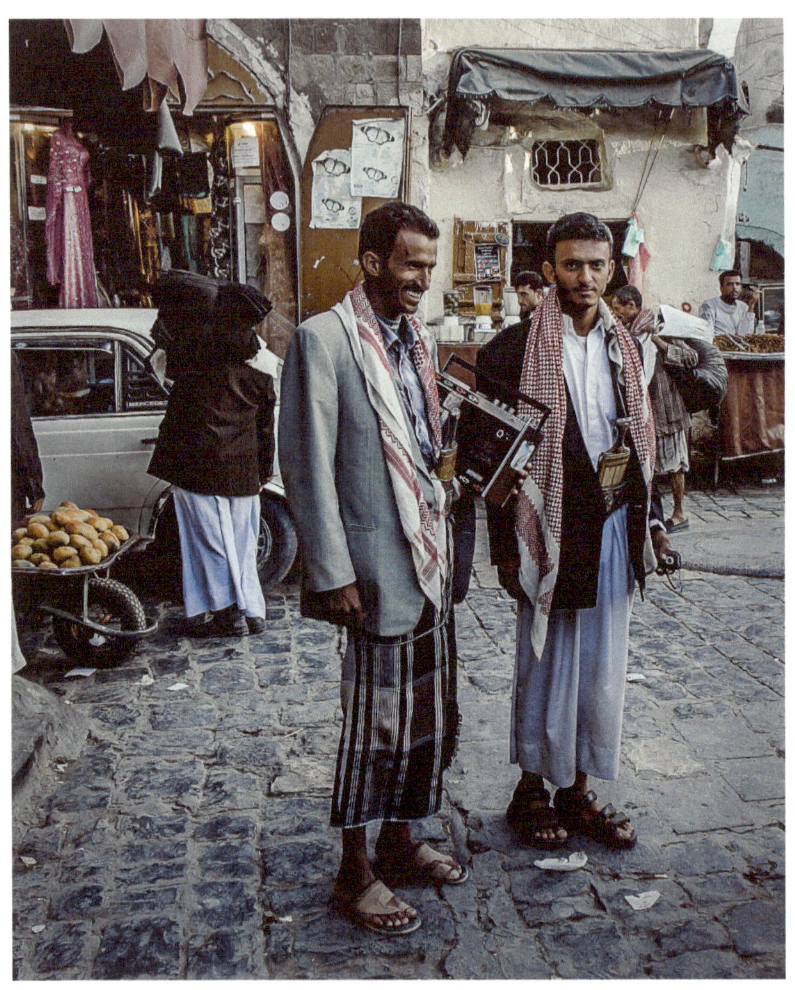

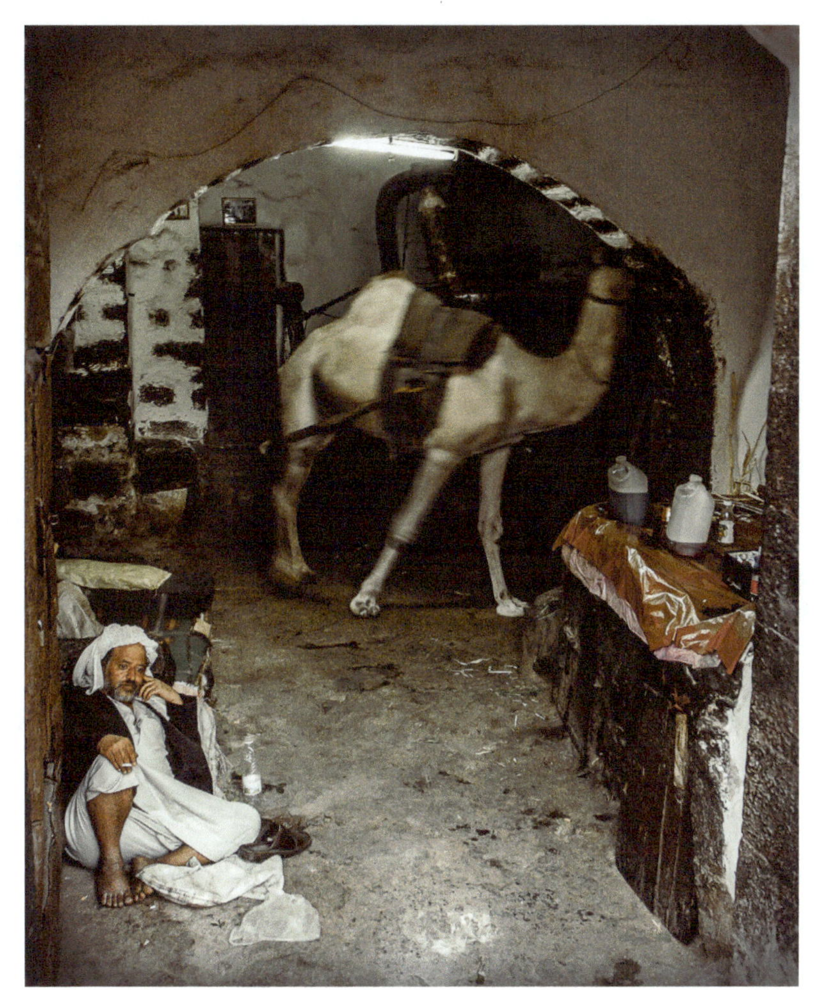

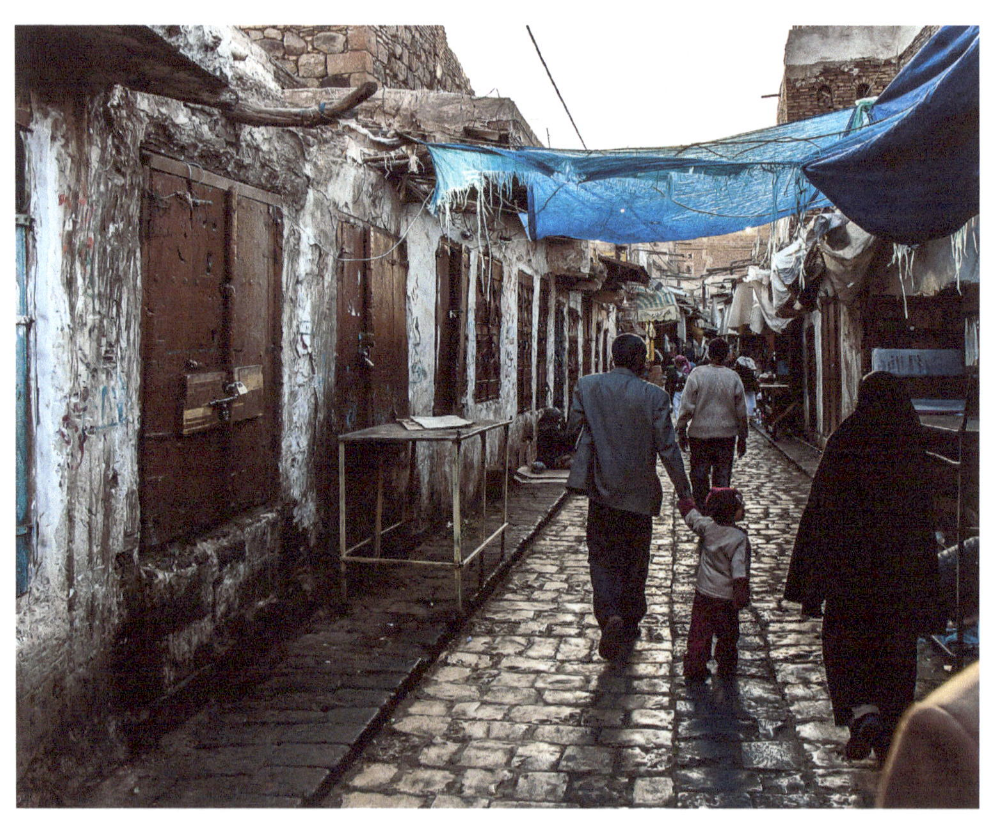

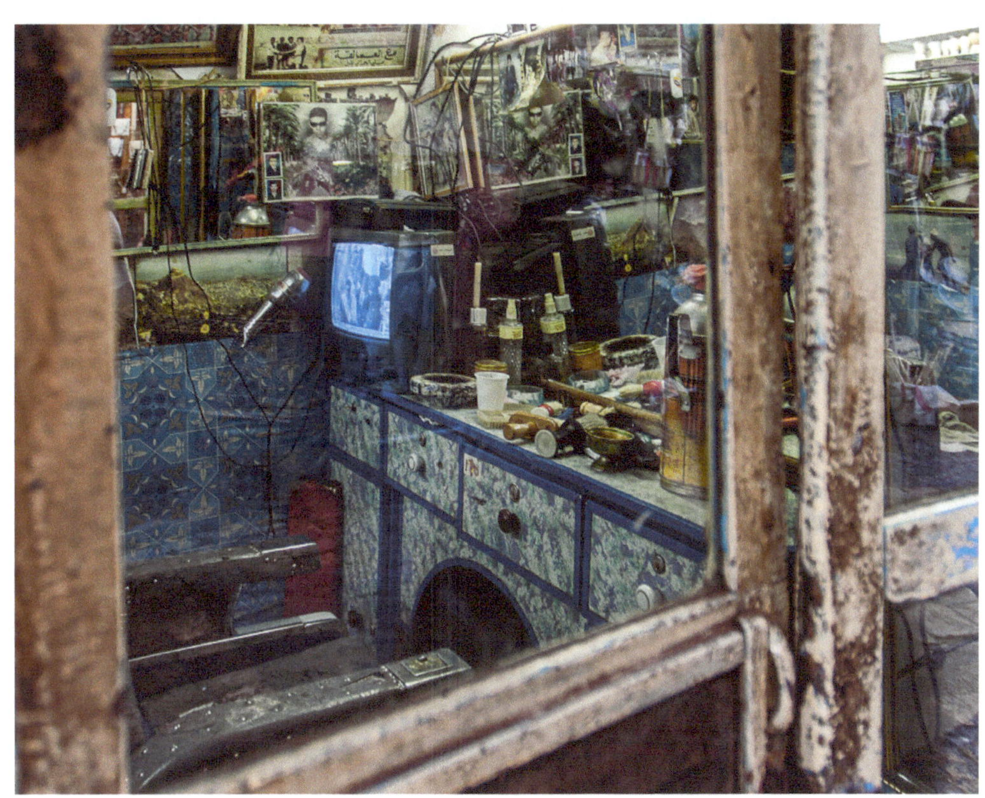

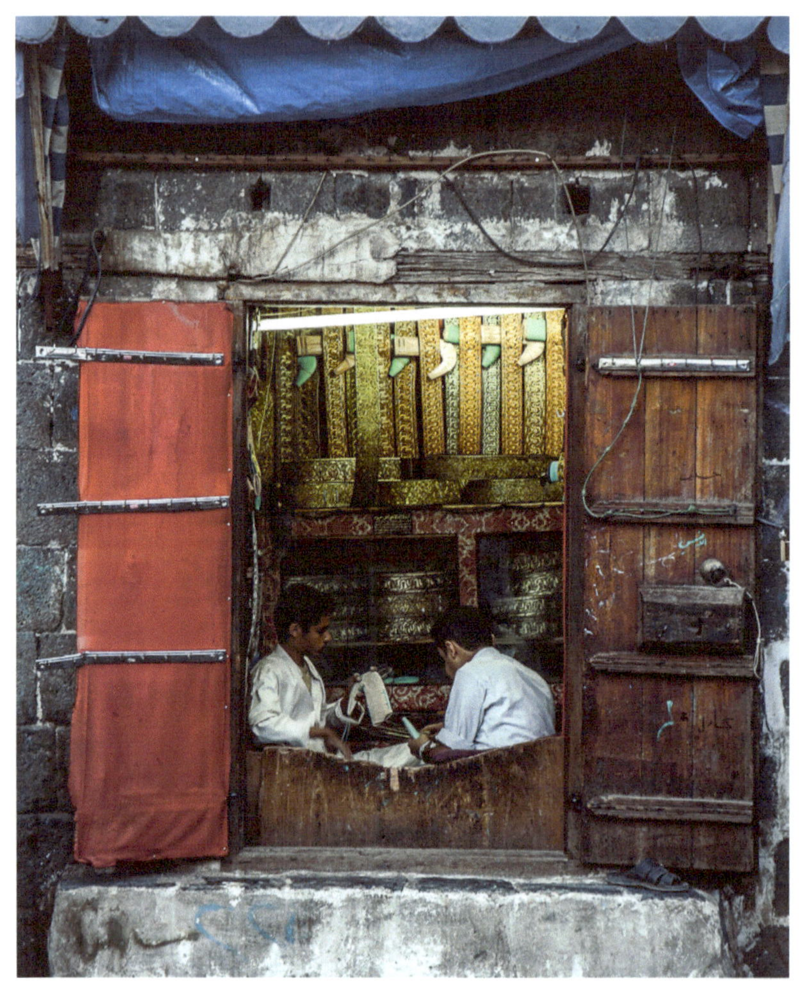

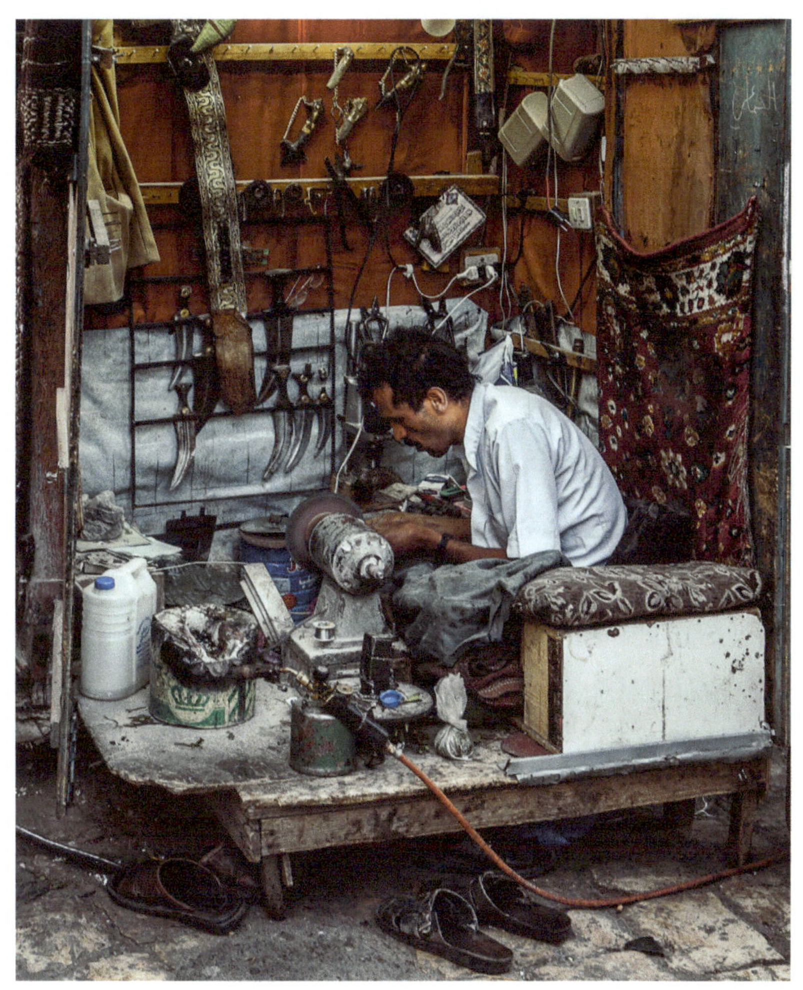

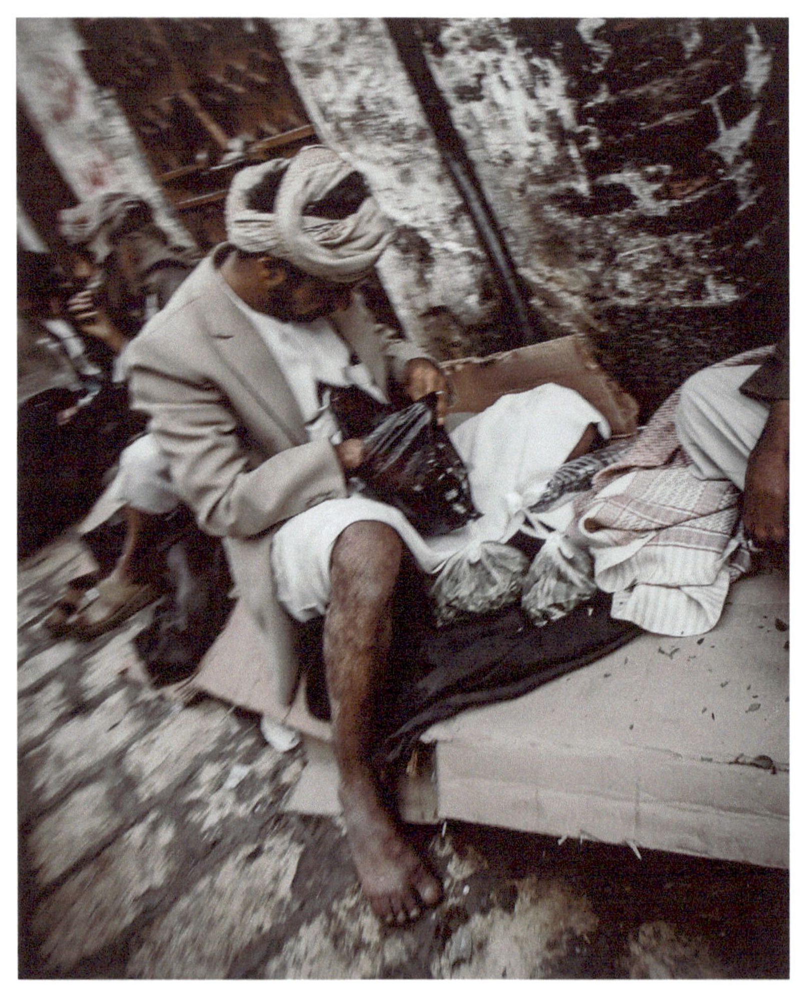

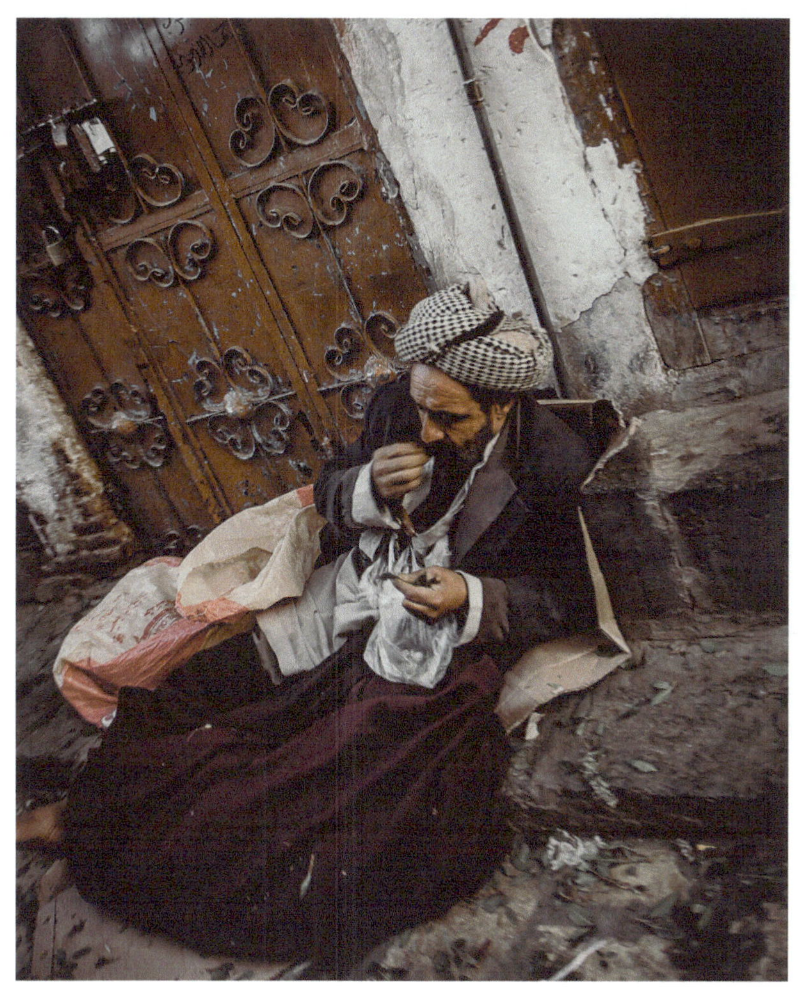

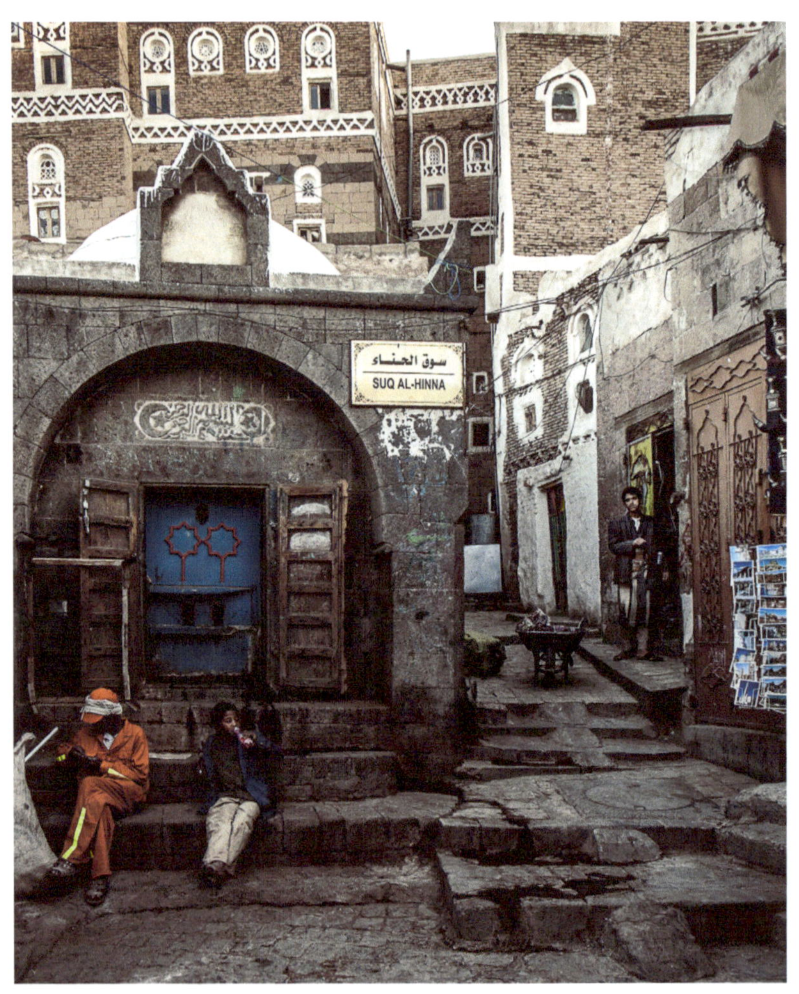
سوق الحناء
SUQ AL-HINNA

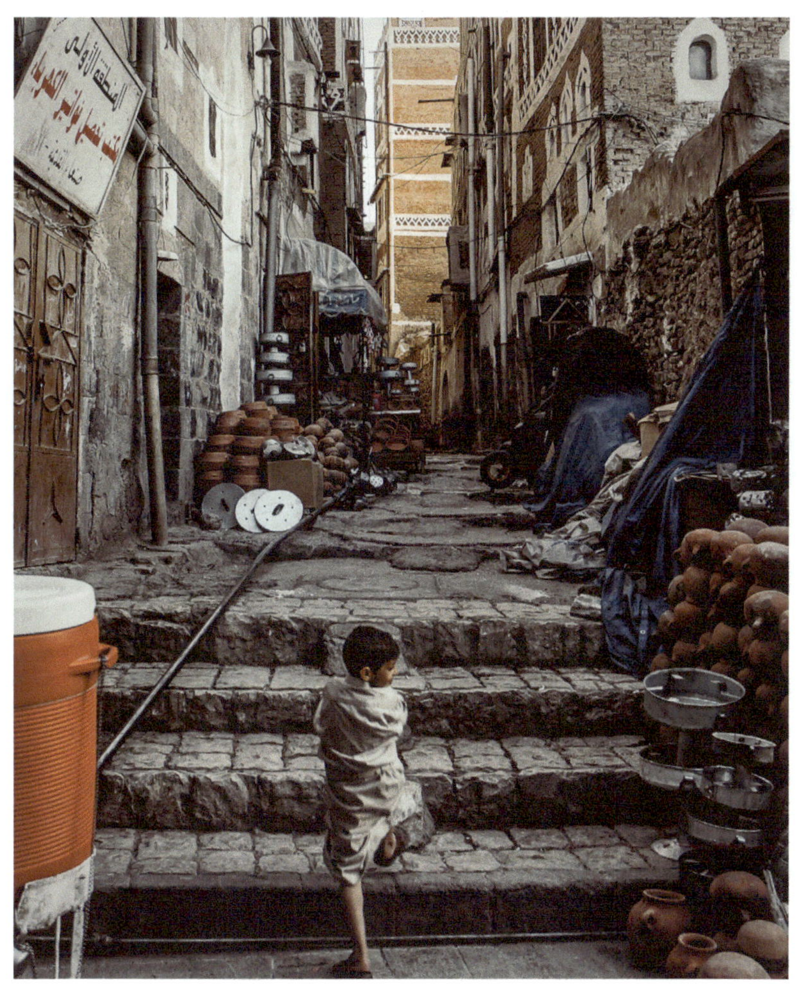

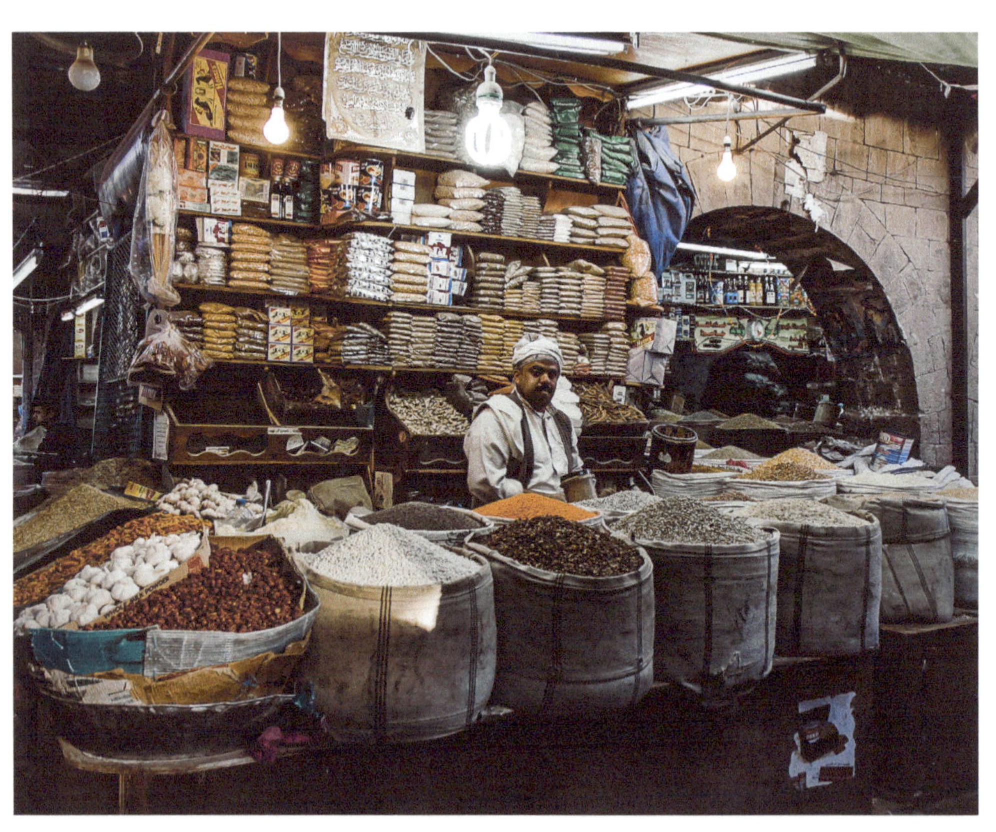

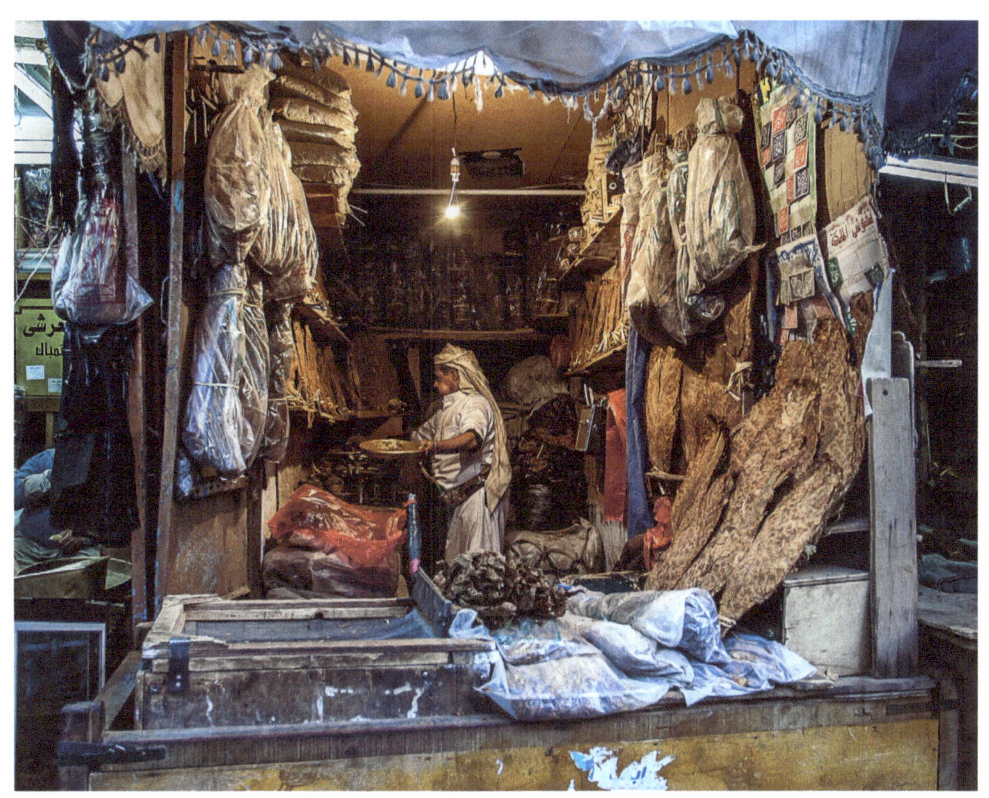

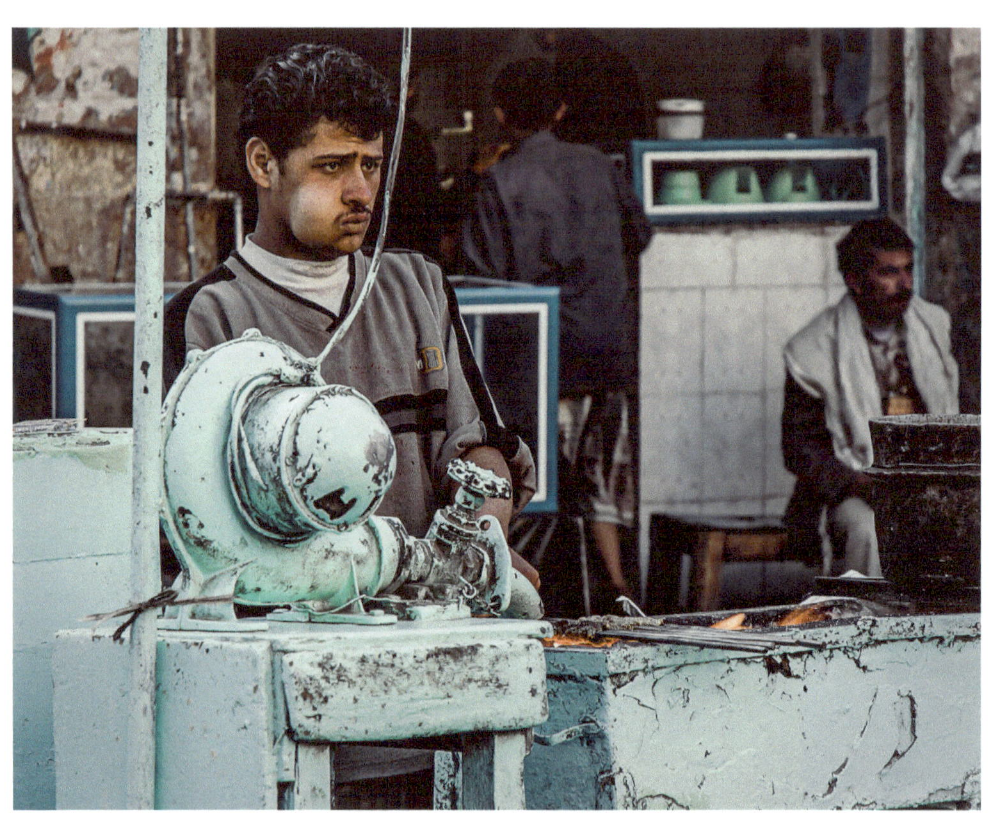

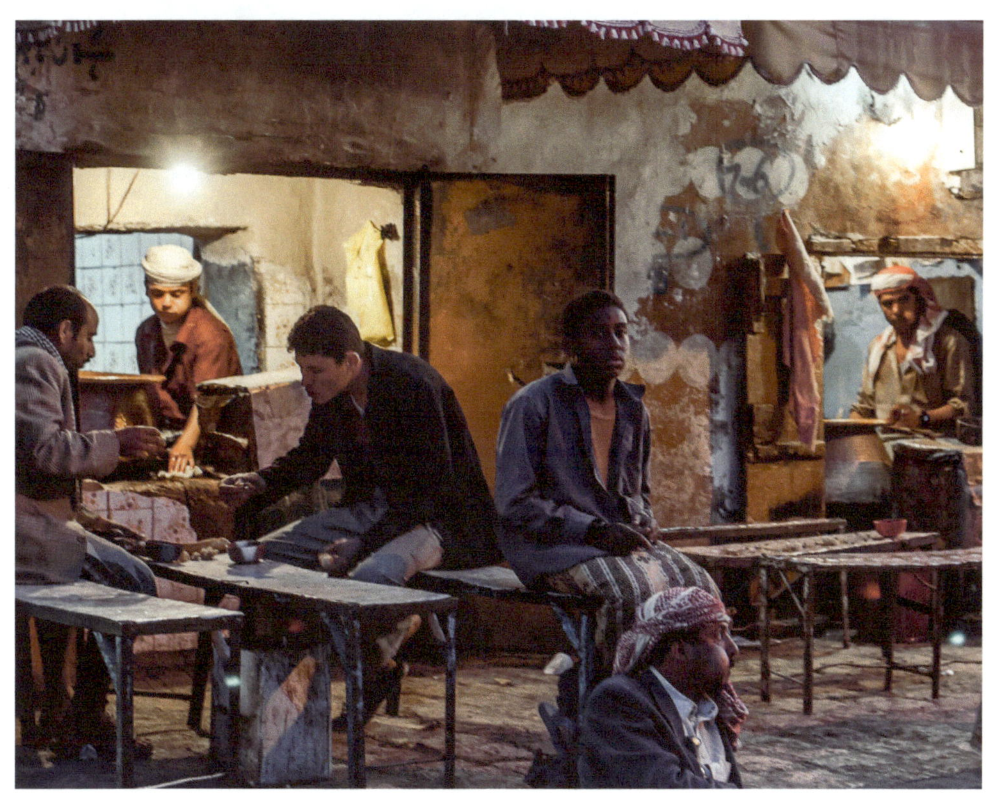

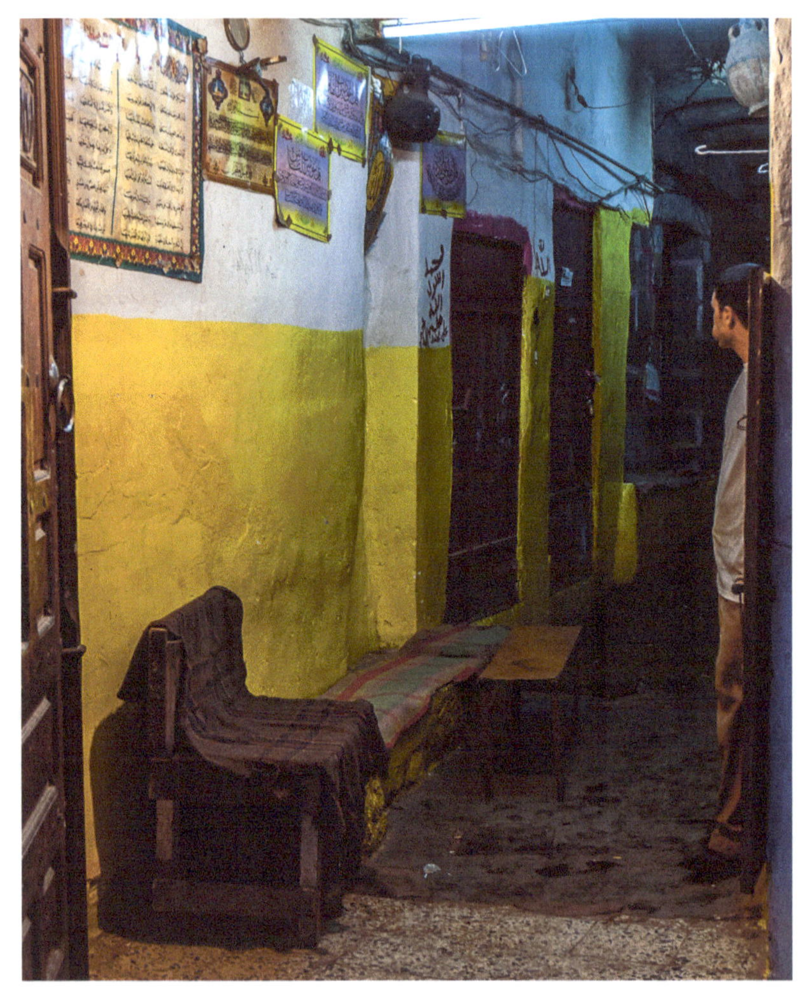

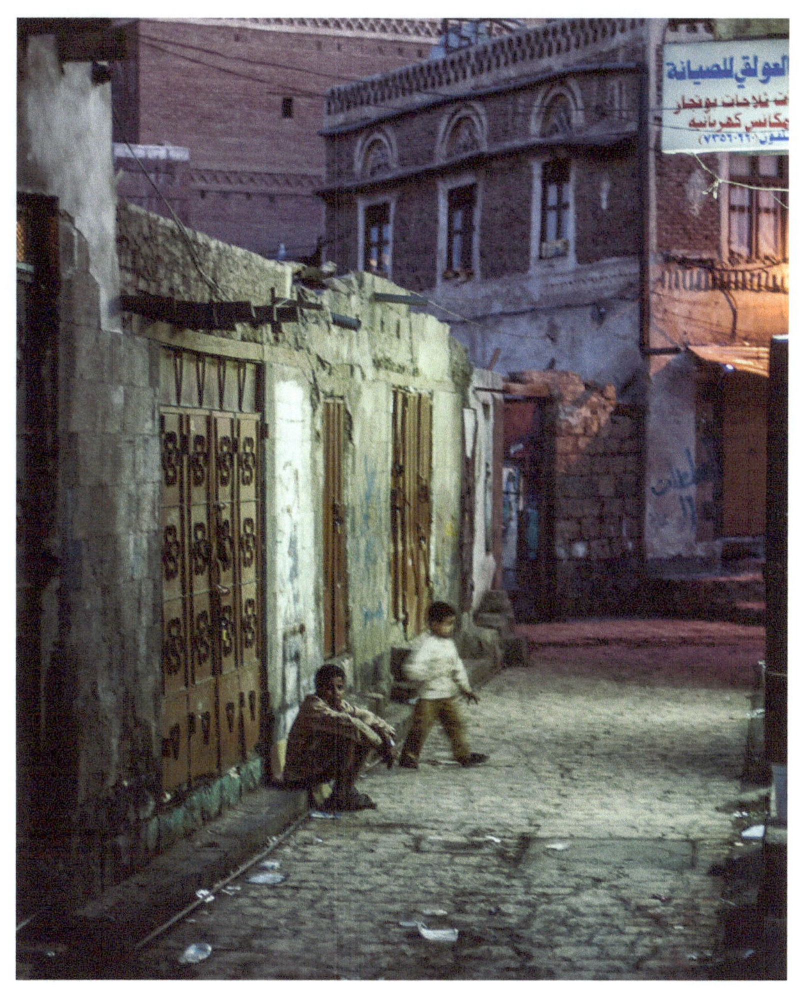
العولقي للصيانة
تلاجات بوتجاز
مكانس كهربائية
تلفون ٧٣٥٦٠٢٠

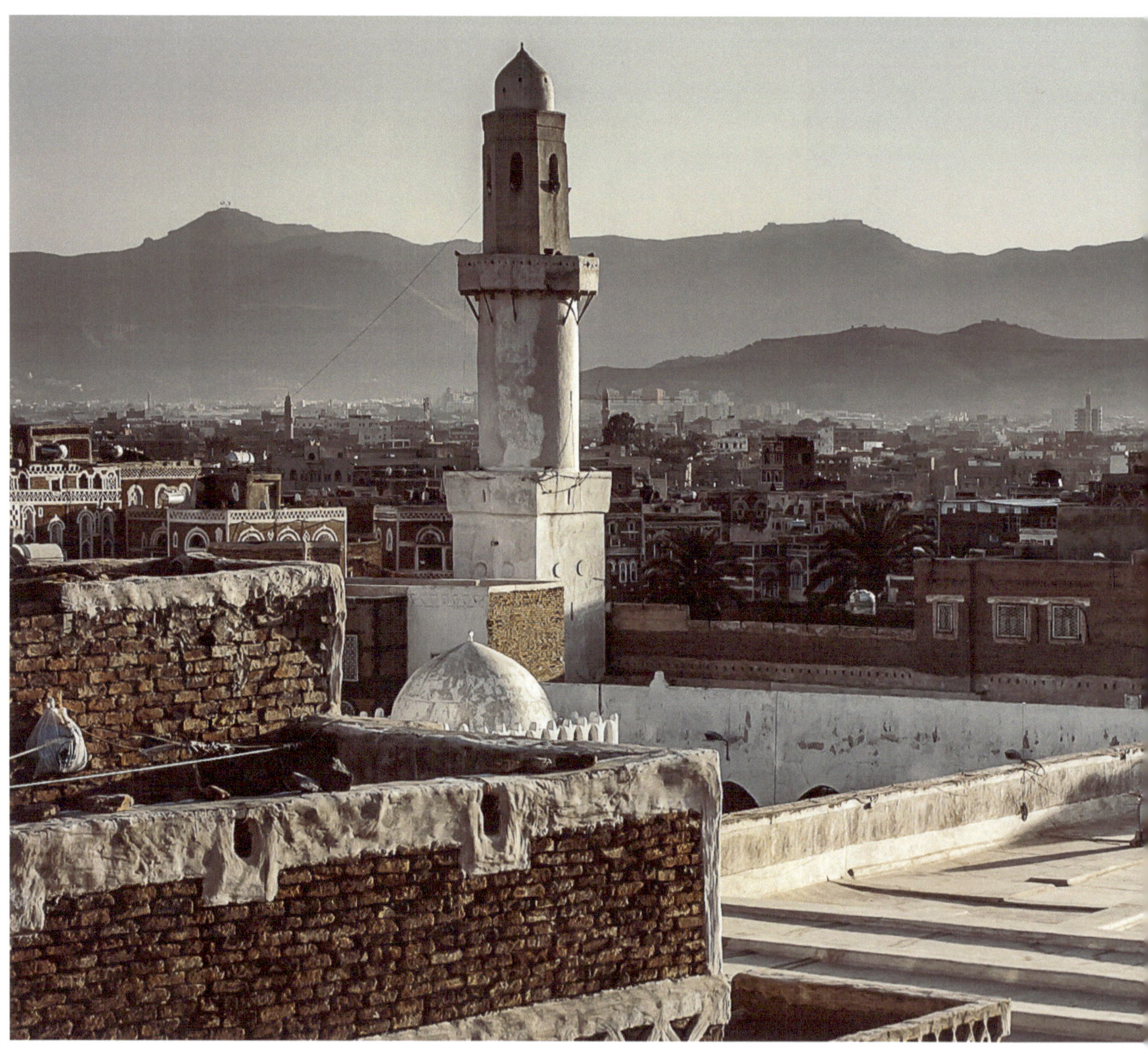

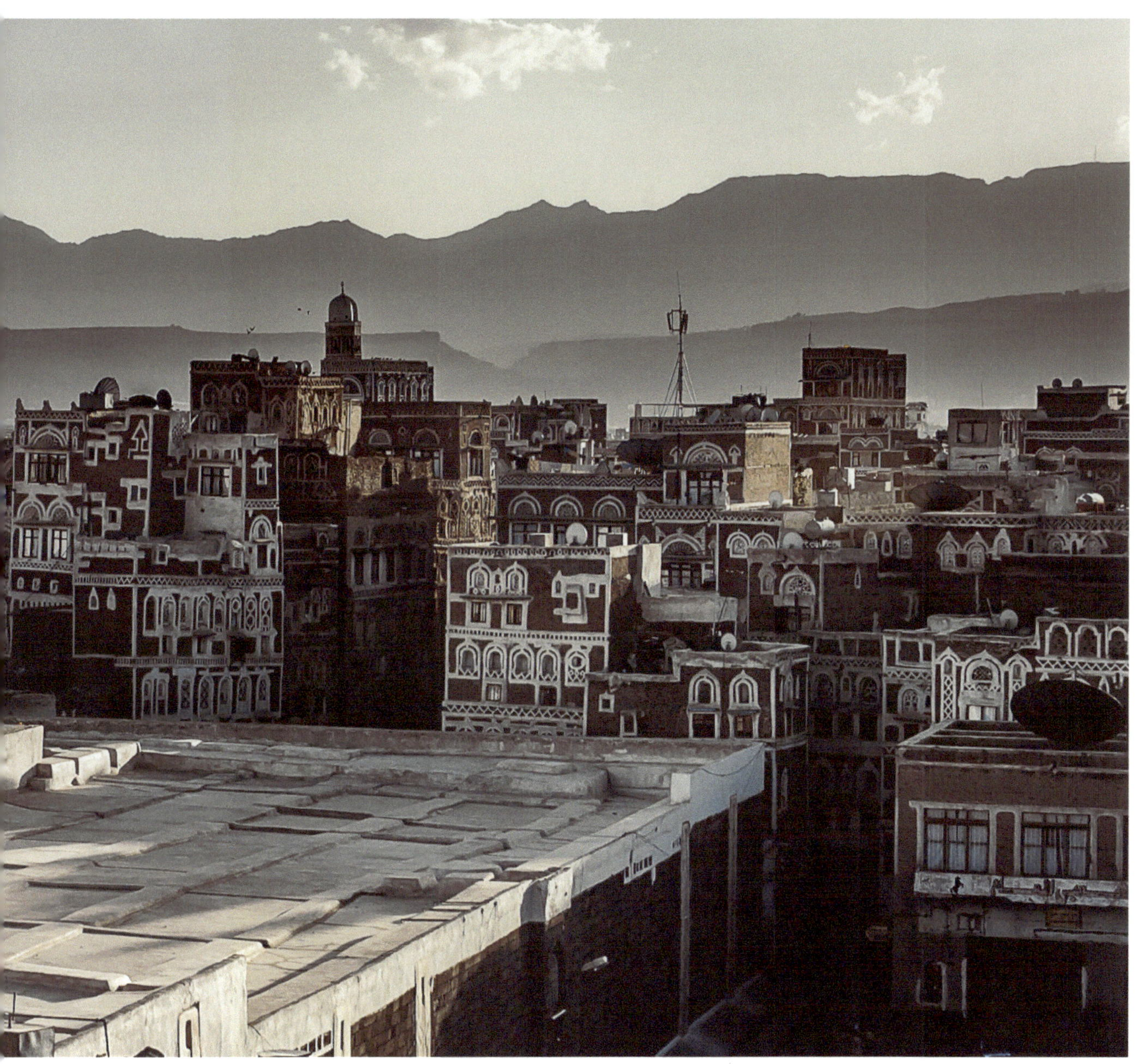

Houssam is a Canadian-Palestinian amateur photographer based in Dubai, UAE.

Although he enjoys digital photography, his passion is in the analog world. He shoots 35mm and medium-format film using mostly mechanical cameras. He self develops, scans and post-processes his work.

He also has full-time jobs as a husband, father, and a senior manager at an enterprise software company.

eMail: hktaha@gmail.com

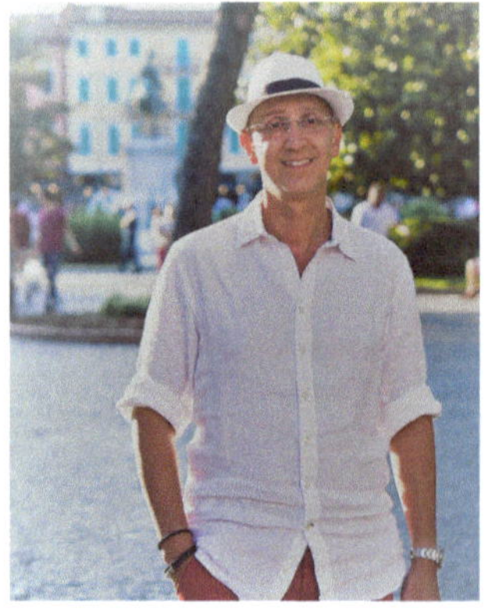